World's Cutest
KITTENS
in 3-D

by Nancy W. Cortelyou

SCHOLASTIC

New York • Toronto • London • Auckland
Sydney • Mexico City • New Delhi • Hong Kong

becker&mayer!
BOOK PRODUCERS

World's Cutest Kittens in 3-D produced by becker&mayer!
11120 NE 33rd Place, Suite 101
Bellevue, WA 98004
www.beckermayer.com

ISBN 978-0-545-43601-4

10 9 8 7 6 5 4 3 2 1   12 13 14 15 16

Printed in Dongguan, China
First edition, January 2012

11832

Written by Nancy W. Cortelyou
Edited by Betsy Henry Pringle
Designed by Megan Sugiyama
Photo research by Katie del Rosario
Production management by Tom Miller
3-D anaglyph effects by Richard Anderson, Matthew Fisher, Cortny Helmick, Joe Mentele, Brandon Walker, Bill Whitaker, and Thumprints Utd Holdings Pte Ltd.
Special thanks to Kiah Helms and Bill Whitaker

Photo credits: Front cover: gray kitten © Anat-oli/Shutterstock; British shorthair kitten © Sasoykc/Dreamstime; red Siberian kitten © dien/Shutterstock. Title page: kittens on stairs © Tomas Mikolands/Shutterstock. Page 3: kitten on orange background © Richard Hözl/Imagebroker.net/Photolibrary. Page 4: sand kitten © Christophe Lehenaff/Photononstop/Photolibrary. Page 5: bobcat kitten © Chris Lorenz/Dreamstime; wild kitten © Twildlife/Dreamstime. Page 6: kittens in basket © Branislav Jovanovic/iStockphoto. Page 7: kitten on windowsill © Paul Reynolds/bigtallguy/Flickr; kitten on fence © Jörgen Larsson/Photolibrary. Page 8: gray fluffy kittens © Michael Krabs/Photolibrary. Page 9: russet kitten in garden © J-L. Klein & M-L. Hubert/Photolibrary; Siamese kitten © Niko Guido/iStockphoto. Page 10: tiny sleeping kitten © Richard Semik/Shutterstock. Page 11: kitten on green cloth © Akira Matoba/Photolibrary; tiny kittens on yellow blanket © Fotosearch/Photolibrary. Page 12: blue-eyed kitten © Victor Burnside/iStockphoto. Page 13: orange kitten © Stefaanh/Dreamstime; Tonkinese kitten © Bill Whitaker. Page 14: white kitten on beach © Oleg Kozlov/Dreamstime. Page 15: Persian kitten © Schulte M/Photolibrary; Donskoy kitten © Anton Gvozdikov/Shutterstock. Page 16: group of kittens © Bartussek I/Photolibrary. Page 17: kittens in basket © Kristian Sekulic/iStockphoto; fuzzy white kittens © Japan Travel Bureau/Photolibrary. Page 18: kitten in tree © Shannon Tidwell/Dreamstime. Page 19: orange kittens exploring © J-L. Klein & M-L. Hubert/Photolibrary; kittens in the wild © AISPIX/Shutterstock. Page 20: kitten in wooden box © Lisa Ison/iStockphoto. Page 21: kitten in pink pocket © Akira Matoba/Superstock/Photolibrary; kitten with teddy bears © Jan Wlodarczyk/The Travel Library/Photolibrary. Page 22: kittens in grass © MartinRugner/Age fotostock/Photolibrary. Page 23: kittens on a walk © Japan Travel Bureau/Photolibrary; kittens on sidewalk © Japan Travel Bureau/Photolibrary. Page 24: Somali kitten © J-L. Klein & M-L. Hubert/Photolibrary. Page 25: Cornish Rex kitten © Vitali Dyatchenko/Dreamstime; cat with tongue © Paul Reynolds/bigtallguy/Flickr. Page 26: kitten with butterfly © cynoclub/iStockphoto. Page 27: white kitten reaching © Tony Campbell/Shutterstock; kitten with soccer ball © Terry Reimink/Shutterstock. Page 28: kittens with big yellow dog © Oya Yalvaç/iStockphoto. Page 29: kitten with sleeping puppy © David Gunn/iStockphoto; kitten and dog in grass © Image Source/Photolibrary. Page 30: tiny kitten in basket © studioimagen/iStockphoto. Page 31: kitten in watering can © David & Micha Sheldon/Photolibrary; orange kitten in garden © Vasiliki Varvaki/iStockphoto. Page 32: smiling kitten © Michael Krabs/Imagebroker.net/Photolibrary. Page 33: gray kitten © PureStock/Photolibrary; Maine coon kitten © jspix jspix/Imagebroker.net/Photolibrary. Page 34: kittens with tree stump © Martin Rugner/Age fotostock/Photolibrary. Page 35: kittens playing in meadow © Martin Rugner/Age fotostock/Photolibrary; kittens in doorway © J-L. Klein & M-L. Hubert/Photolibrary. Page 36: kitten hanging from a branch © J-L. Klein & M-L. Hubert/Photolibrary. Page 37: kitten in tree © B. Stefanov/Dreamstime; kitten in apple tree © Tatiana Morozova/Dreamstime. Page 38: kitten in bucket © Pat Powers & Cherryl Schafer/Photolibrary. Page 39: mama sphynx and kitten © Jacqueline Hunkele/iStockphoto; fuzzy kitten bathing © cath5/Shutterstock. Page 40: group of Maine coon kittens © Linn Currie/iStockphoto. Page 41: kittens in flowerpots © Michael Krabs/Imagebroker.net/Photolibrary; kitten in scarf © Juniors Bildarchiv/Photolibrary. Page 42: silly cat with family © Creativ Studio Heinemann/Photolibrary. Page 43: Siamese kitten and whippet puppy © Juniors Bildarchiv/Photolibrary; funny gray kitten © Igor Sokolov/Dreamstime. Page 44: kittens in hay © Lothar Lenz/Photolibrary. Page 45: kitten with cow © Hans Reinhard/Photolibrary; kitten with chicks © Bruno Mathieu/Photolibrary. Page 46: kitten peeking out of window © Mitsuaki Iwago/Minden Pictures/National Geographic Stock. Page 47: kittens peeking out of fence © Tony Campbell/iStockphoto; kitten in pipe © J-L. Klein © M-L. Hubert/Photolibrary. Page 48: Russian blue kitten © MIXA Co. Ltd./Photolibrary. Back cover: Bengal kitten © Utekhina Anna/Shutterstock; yawning tabby © Norman Chan/Dreamstime; kitten pair © Andreykuzmin/Dreamstime; kitten with ball © Mnogosmyslov Aleksey/Dreamstime; sleeping kitten © Ira Bachinskaya/iStockphoto.

Here, kitty, kitty!

What could be cuter than a soft and cuddly kitten? *Lots* of soft and cuddly kittens! These tiny bundles of fur come in a variety of colors and patterns. Kittens love to hide, pounce, climb, and chase—but they are not just playing when they do these things. They are practicing skills they will use when they grow up.

Do you want to find out more about adorable kittens? Punch out and put together the 3-D glasses inside the front cover of this book. Then get ready to go nose-to-nose with the world's cutest kittens!

Hello! I'm ready to play. Are you?

Wildcats

Did I see something yummy run into the bushes?

Mousetrap

Wildcats became house cats because of mice! About 10,000 years ago, farmers began storing grain. The piles of grain attracted mice. Small wildcats started hanging around the granaries, looking for a meal. The farmers didn't like the mice, so they were glad to have the cats. In time, the wildcats got used to being around people.

Walk on the wild side

Wildcats from the Middle East are the ancestors of all modern house cats. If you saw one of these wildcats, you might think it was a full-grown striped tabby. This kitten is a North American wildcat called a bobcat. Bobcats are named for their short "bobbed" tails.

I look pretty big standing on this log, don't I?

Wild thing

Like their house cat cousins, wildcat kittens depend on their mothers for food. Once the kittens are ready for solid food, the mother teaches them to hunt. She brings prey back to the nest so the babies can practice catching it. Bobcat kittens remain with their mother until they are about a year old.

Where's Mom? I'm hungry!

Short-haired and Sweet

Let's go on the count of three. One . . . two . . . three!

Mouse hunters

Who hitched a ride to America on the *Mayflower*? American shorthairs! Or, at least, their European ancestors did. Then they found their way west during the California gold rush. American shorthairs were popular with the early settlers, who paid as much as $50 apiece for these strong-jawed mouse hunters.

Tabbies

Tabby refers to the pattern of a cat's coat, not a breed. The two main tabby types are mackerel and classic. Mackerels have thin stripes. Classic tabbies have wide stripes and swirls or circles on their sides. Tabbies have white "eyeliner" around their eyes and they often have an *M* on their forehead.

If you come closer, I'll tell you a secret.

Can that nice fireman get me down from here?

It's a boy!

Until a kitten is about three weeks old, it can be hard to tell if it's a male or a female. Its orange coat signals that this tabby is most likely a male. Orange tabbies are more often male than female. Calicoes—white cats with orange and black patches—are usually female.

Balls of Fluff

Hey, one of those clouds looks like a mouse!

Five wegies

Norwegian Forest kittens first lived in the cold forests of Norway. Thick double coats keep them cozy and warm. Wegies, as they are called, have large, round feet with tufts of fur between their toes. It takes these puffy pusses five years to reach their full size. Wegies always use their inside voices. That's because they are born with a quiet meow!

Garden gnome

Fluffy, round-eyed Persians are one of the most popular cat breeds in the United States. They used to be called longhairs—a suitable name for cats that need to be brushed every day. The especially thick hair around a Persian's face is called a ruff.

My owner thinks I'm the cutest kitten ever. Do you?

What's the point?

Siamese kittens are born white. They develop the dark markings of a Siamese, called points, as they get older. According to legend, Siamese cats once guarded the royal family of Siam, now called Thailand. These days, anyone can own one of these talkative, playful, active cats. Siamese cats can be long-haired or short-haired.

Can you see me? I'm as white and fluffy as the carpet!

Itty-bitty Kitties

I think I'll take a little rest right here.

A little shut-eye

A kitten is born with its eyes closed. When it is one week old, the eyes start to open. It takes several more days before both of them are open and working properly. A kitten's vision is blurry at first. It continues to get stronger after both eyes are open.

Tickle my tummy, Mom

A newborn kitten is helpless without its mother. For the first two weeks, it is nearly deaf and blind, and it needs to nurse every few hours. The mother grooms the kitten with her tongue, feeds it, and helps it go to the bathroom.

How about a hug?

Warm and cozy

Keeping warm is an important part of a kitten's early weeks. It isn't able to control its own body heat, so it stays close to its mother. These two itty-bitty kitties are staying warm and cozy in a blanket while they wait for Mom to return.

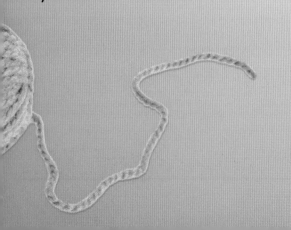

Let's cuddle here until Mom comes back.

Blue-eyed Babies

Here I am, ready or not.

Baby's got blue eyes

Just like many human babies, most kittens are born with blue eyes. As they develop, the color changes. By the time a kitten is three months old, its eye color is set. Typical eye colors are gold, green, copper, and blue. No matter what color their eyes are, most cats don't have eyelashes!

Sense of sight

Cats are not color blind, but they don't see the world the same way people do. The shades in their world are mostly blues and greens. And they are able to see in the dark better than humans can. Their big pupils open up wide for excellent night vision. This is helpful because cats are most active at night.

I'm coming to get you.

Whatcha doing?

Kittens for life

This little kitten is Tonkinese. It will get bigger, but cats in this breed tend to act like kittens their whole lives. They love to invent games and play fetch. Tonkinese cats look similar to Siamese cats. This breed is known for its aquamarine eyes, but some Tonks have blue, green, or yellow-green eyes.

Funny Faces

Hiss! This sand makes my feet itch!

King of the house

Although this little kitten looks fierce, a Cornish Rex is actually friendly and playful. It is adventurous and kittenlike its whole life. This breed is known for its big ears and short, fuzzy down coat. A Rex prefers to stay indoors to keep warm. Maybe that's why this one looks so mad!

Lap blanket

A Persian would rather curl up in your lap than do anything else. Maybe it's because their short legs make it hard for these cats to run and jump. Many people consider these flat-faced felines a favorite. Other people think the faces look squished. What do you think?

My, what a big forehead I have!

Sweater girl

Even when it's newborn, a Donskoy kitten has wrinkles. Like kittens in other hairless breeds, this one isn't completely hair free—it has supershort downy fur. The Donskoy has monkeylike paws that can grab things more easily than the paws of other kinds of cat can.

Even my wrinkles have wrinkles!

Furry Families

Mommy, come join us!

Kitty needs a name

Mother cats don't get to name their babies. People do. But how do you choose? Fluffy, Tiger, or Grizzabella? Some people believe a cat can learn its name and will come when it's called. Cat experts say that for the best results, it's helpful to give a kitten a name that ends in an *ee* sound.

Brothers and sisters

A litter of kittens is a bunch of brothers and sisters born at the same time. Four to six kittens in a litter is typical. The most ever was nineteen! Sometimes the kittens in a litter have different fathers, so the kittens don't all look the same.

Scoot over! Let's make room for Twinkle!

Furry foursome

Himalayan kitties are a mix of two other breeds, Persian and Siamese. They grow into flat-faced, short-legged, long-haired fluff balls like Persians. But they have colored points like Siamese. Himalayans love to stay indoors and be groomed.

Who wants to go outside when you can snuggle on the sofa?

On the Prowl

I'm paws-itively stuck!

This one's a handful

A kitten's front paws have four toes and a "thumb," called the dewclaw, higher up on the paw. The back paws have four toes and no dewclaw. It is common for kittens to be born with extra toes—usually on the front feet. No matter how many toes a kitten has, it can quickly get itself up a tree and into trouble!

Catwalk

Cats walk on tiptoe. A walking cat steps with both left legs, then both right legs. Other animals that walk this way are giraffes and camels. When a cat trots, its gait changes, and it moves with alternating left and right legs together. When running, a cat is propelled by its two hind legs pushing off at the same time.

Left, left, right, right.

Playing with your food

Curious kittens love to explore the world, just as their ancestors did. They are attracted to the movement of their prey. If a kitten catches a mouse or other rodent, it might bat the animal around long after it's captured. The cat is playing with its food because it is wary that the food might fight back.

Two heads are better than one. Don't you think, brother?

Catnaps

Purr-fectly content

After a big day of exploring, this little kitty needs a nap! A hollowed-out fence post is just the spot. Contented kittens purr themselves to sleep. With each breath, air passes through folds in the voice box inside a kitten's throat. This creates the purr sound you hear. Cats also purr to communicate and when they are ill or feeling stressed.

Exploring is hard work!

Dream weaver

Kittens and cats have lots of energy when they are awake. But they spend only about four hours a day actually moving around. The rest of the time they rest or sleep. A kitten will start dreaming when it is one week old. What do you think kittens dream about?

I'm getting my beauty sleep. . . .

I love sleepovers with my friends.

I knead you!

A kitten presses its front paws up and down to knead, or massage, its mother's belly. This helps stimulate the flow of milk. When a kitten grows up, it will do the same thing to its owner's stomach—or to any soft spot where it wants to take a nap.

First Friends

You're my sister AND my best friend.

Tiger-striped love

A kitten's brothers and sisters are its first friends. Siblings keep one another entertained and out of trouble. When littermates are playing together, they are learning social skills—the ways they need to behave in order to get along with other cats.

On the boardwalk

When they are about three weeks old, kittens start playing with their siblings. They form groups and have favorites. Not all cats get along with one another. But these two curious kitties definitely see eye-to-eye.

Let's run as fast as we can. Ready . . . set . . .

New kittens on the block

Tall grass and leafy bushes attract kittens. Why? Because a mouse might be hiding in the shadows! These two friends are working together in their hunt. One is looking for dinner. The other is keeping watch for nosy, noisy dogs.

I hear something! I smell something!

Super Senses

I said, STOP TICKLING ME!

Whiskers!

Whiskers give a kitten a superior sense of touch. A cat or kitten has whiskers around its mouth, above its eyes, and behind its paws. Whisker hairs are highly sensitive. If a kitty's whiskers touch the edge of its food bowl, the kitten might paw food out of the bowl and eat it off the floor instead.

Ears!

Because cats are hunters, their ears can detect sounds that humans can't hear. Each ear can swivel in the direction of a sound. A cat also uses its ears to show how it feels. If the ears point up, the kitten is relaxed and happy. If the ears lie flat against the head, the kitten is afraid. And if the ears are turned backward, you've got one angry cat. Beware!

Did I hear the can opener?

Look, Ma! My tongue is as long as my whiskers!

Tongues!

A lick from a cat can feel like being swiped with sandpaper. That's because a cat's tongue is covered with tiny, hooklike bumps. These "hooks" help the kitten smooth its fur and get every bit of meat off a bone. A cat's tongue can lap, or scoop up, liquid as fast as four times per second.

25

Summer Fun

Come back. I just want to play.

Butterfly catcher

All cats are hunters, and hunting lessons start when cats are kittens. A kitten may sit and wait for its prey. Or it may stalk and then run after it. A kitten will also hide and then pounce on another kitten, its owner's feet, or anything else that moves. To a kitten, hunting and playing are the same thing.

Standing on your own two feet

If you hold a toy above a kitten's head, it might stand on two feet and try to reach the toy with its front paws. A standing cat supports itself on strong hind legs. Strong leg muscles and a flexible spine allow a cat to jump as high as five times its own height!

Let's dance!

Game time!

Everything is a toy for a kitten. If the toy makes noise or moves, it's even better! If you have a kitten, make sure you have lots of kitty-safe toys for it to play with. Otherwise, your kitten may decide to attack and play with something you don't want it to.

Which way is the goal?

Puppy Pals

Don't worry, Rover. I'll protect you!

Sweethearts

Despite their differences, cats and dogs can be good friends. Dogs are social creatures—they like to play with and be around others. Kittens are more independent. However, when Mom isn't nearby, a dog can be a warm, cozy stand-in for cuddling.

Childhood friends

Kittens need to spend more time with their mothers than puppies do. A two-month-old pup is ready to become part of your family. Kittens shouldn't be adopted until they are about four months old. Cats and dogs can be friends, but it's best if they meet when they are young.

We'll always be best friends, right?

Like cats and dogs

Wet noses are usually a sign of good health for both cats and dogs. When a dog wags its tail, it is a sign of happiness. A friendly cat holds its tail upright, like this one. If a cat is unhappy with a dog, watch out! It will puff up its tail, hiss, and even scratch.

I smell tuna. Have you been eating my food?

Shh! I'm Hiding!

This is cozy. Maybe a little *too* cozy!

Hide-and-seek

Newborn kittens weigh about 3 ounces—less than the weight of a stick of butter! Even as it grows, a kitten sometimes likes to wriggle into cozy places. Maybe it is playing a friendly game of hide-and-seek, or maybe it just needs some time alone.

I'm a spy!

Peekaboo!

A kitten is curious. You never know where you will find one hiding. Because cats like to sneak up on their prey, hiding is step number one in the hunt. When a kitty seems to appear from out of nowhere, it was probably hiding and getting ready to pounce on its prey. Or on your ankles!

All turned around

A kitten is able to twist itself into odd positions and creep into tiny spaces because it has narrow shoulders and no collarbone. The bones in a cat's spine are loosely connected, so its backbone is extremely flexible.

Which way was I going?

Hear Me Roar!

I'm kind of fierce, aren't I?

King of the jungle

This kitten looks like it is practicing to be a big, roaring lion. But house cats can't roar. They can hiss. When a kitten hisses, it arches its back to make itself look bigger and meaner. The kitty is trying to scare the thing that is threatening it.

The cat's meow

When a kitten wants something, it meows. This gets the attention of its mother, its owner, and other animals. A cat rarely meows at other cats. Cats can't put together their lips to make the M sound in *meow*. The sound they are really making is *eeow*.

Yarrrrrgh! I'm a pirate.

Now hear this!

A howling success

Perched like a lion on a mountaintop, this Maine coon kitten is letting its voice be heard. If you hear a cat howl, the sound may mean the animal is injured or upset. Some cats howl just to get attention. It usually works!

Playing Rough

Smells like home

Every cat has its own territory, or area, that it defends from intruders. By leaving a special scent mark on the ground, trees, and even furniture, a cat tells other cats and kittens, "I was here and this is mine."

This is MY stump!

Wrestling with affection

A kitten learns by watching its mother and playing with its brothers and sisters. It practices hunting and wrestling moves through play. When a kitten needs a break from the roughhousing, you might hear a hiss. To your corners, kitties!

Had enough?

Scratch attack

A kitten's claws are made from the same material—keratin—that your fingernails are. And they are always growing and replacing themselves. Unlike a dog's claws, which are always out, a cat's claws are hidden until the paw is extended.

Hey, that's my ear!

Up a Tree!

Look out below!

Hanging from a limb

Sometimes what attracts a kitten to a tree is a bird or a squirrel. Without thinking, the kitten climbs to the top branches, chasing a meal! If a kitten gets trapped, it will either jump out of the tree or realize that heading back down tail first is the way back to solid ground.

Tree hugger

Cats like high places where they can keep an eye on you but not be seen. This makes any secluded perch a favorite, whether it's a tree branch or the top of the refrigerator. Climbing up high is also a good way for a kitten to get away from a dog that is chasing it!

Can they see me up here?

This apple tree is a real pickle!

Friends in high places

Cats are good climbers—as long as they are climbing UP! Kitty claws curve forward and point downward. These let a kitten climb easily to the highest part of a tree. It's another story when the kitty is ready to climb down. Its claws are curved the wrong way. To grasp the bark, the kitty must shimmy down the tree tail first.

37

Clean Kitties

I better get a good treat for putting up with this!

Ready. Set. Wet!

Most cats don't like water, although some are fascinated by a dripping faucet or the bathroom shower. No matter what you do, it's hard to get a cat to take a bath or go swimming. Cats seem to prefer their own method of grooming.

Mommy and me

Kittens start life with a ready-made groomer—Mom! The mother cat's gentle licks not only clean the newborn, they help it start breathing, nurse, and go to the bathroom. Grooming soothes the kitten and helps it bond with its mother.

Oh, Mom, that tickles.

Cleaning machine

Kittens quickly learn how to groom themselves. Grooming gives the kitten healthy skin and fur, helps it stay cool in the summer and warm in the winter, and removes scents that came from food or humans. Cats also calm themselves by grooming.

Now I smell like ME again!

Picture Perfect

We're supermodels!

A full house

This feline family is big in more ways than one. Maine coon cats are from New England. These gentle giants are one of the tallest cat breeds, and they weigh the most. A full-grown male can be 20 pounds. That's as heavy as two bowling balls!

Three little kittens

Some people like to take photos of their pets dressed up in funny clothing or in odd places. Some cats like photo sessions, some don't. Either way, it's hard to get a good shot in which all the cats are smiling and looking at the camera at the same time. Just like with people!

We've lost our mittens!

I was playing with a ball of yarn, and look what happened!

It's a string thing

This kitty is wearing a knitted scarf as it poses for a holiday portrait. Kittens love yarn. It's soft and stringy and fun to play with, especially when it comes unraveled. A kitten will pounce on a woolly ball of yarn and bat it around like it is a mouse. Don't expect your kitty to knit a scarf, though!

Picture—
Not So Perfect!

There's one in every family!

Purr-sonality plus

The way a kitten is treated during its first few weeks can affect its personality for life. The more handling a kitten experiences between the ages of four and twelve weeks of age, the friendlier it will be. Still, even though kittens from the same litter often share the same experiences, they can end up with very different personalities.

Funny face

Look at that sneer! It's what happens when a cat sniffs an especially interesting smell. The kitten curls back its upper lip and breathes in. This pulls the scent to an area on the roof of the mouth that can "taste" the smell. This response, called flehmen, is something horses do as well.

Who said you could sit here?

Split personality

Most cats seem to have more than one personality. One minute, your kitten is purring happily in your lap. The next minute, it bites you and runs away. One minute, your kitten is the picture of elegance and grace. The next minute, it is making a silly face for the camera!

I'm perfectly fine. Really!

Farm Friends

Hey, what's over there?

Barn kitties

Kittens that live on farms make good mousers! Their soft, padded paws help make them silent hunters. Their keen sense of hearing lets them hear the sounds of mice scratching from behind walls.

Mom power

If a kitten is taken away from its mother or mothering cat too soon, it might get attached to a new mom. That mother doesn't even have to be a cat—there are lots of other possibilities on a farm! A kitten needs about four months with its mother and siblings to learn the ways of the world.

That's the spot!

One, two, three . . . wait! Where's Mike?

Please touch!

A barn kitten like this one can be a friend and protector to other animals on the farm. But unless a kitten is handled and petted by people when it is young, it will grow up to be afraid of new people, new animals, and new things. It's best if a kitten is handled a lot during its first six weeks of life.

Here Comes Trouble!

Mischief maker

Curiosity plus boredom equals trouble for a kitten! Solo kittens often get themselves into mischief. Some like to chew and claw stuffed animals or furniture. Others get tangled in cords. Most cats are able to leap long distances, often jumping up into—and sometimes out of—window frames. Perhaps they just want to be where they can see what's going on outside.

Did I just hear the ice-cream-truck bell?

A nose for news

A cat's sensitive nose detects scents that humans can't smell. Just a whiff can warn a kitten that a dog is nearby. Some people say cats are finicky eaters because they sniff their food before they eat it. The cat is just making sure its dinner is safe to eat.

Do you smell something? I do!

In and out of trouble

It's impossible to know what this little troublemaker is up to! Is it coming out of the pipe or did it back itself in? Either way, you can be sure the kitten was curious about something it smelled, heard, or saw. Maybe the kitty thought the pipe was a giant mouse hole and was hoping to find a giant mouse!

Well, this is embarrassing!

Gimme five!

Always adorable

Kittens come in all colors and sizes, and each kitten has its own personality. Some kittens are shy, others want to follow you and play, and some like to attack everything they see! Kittens are independent, but they still need to be part of a loving family.

Long-haired, short-haired, or no-haired, all house cats have a little wildcat in them. With so many adorable kittens to choose from, which kitten is YOUR favorite?